"There are more things to life and understanding than we are currently unable to accept or process. One day we will understand and have a greater knowledge of them but until then we just have to make of things what we can."

The Paranormal
Things that go bump in the night.

Drew Martin

contents

THE PARANORMAL!

 OOh! Ghosts and weird stuff! I have always had a fascination with this subject. Am I a believer? Well, that is for me to know! What we do have is an opportunity to look at things and ask questions. The perfect subject for exercising the brain!

 To do this we have to keep an open mind and tell ourselves we have an open mind. Most of the time there is always a logical explanation but sometimes? Well, that is for the individual to decide. What you can't do is just dismiss things because of your beliefs. Once again view things with an open mind. Remember, Once you eliminate the impossible, whatever remains, no matter how improbable must be the truth (Sir Arthur Conan Doyle)

 There are many reasons why people believe

in the supernatural. In the most part, it is down to mankind's need to fill a gap in their minds where there is a lack of understanding or knowledge. It is the need to have something else in life that drives us towards a belief or passion in any chosen subject. The need to be part of a group of like-minded people so we don't feel alone.

Chapter 1

Why do we believe?

"There has to be a reason" is often the response we hear. The fact is there is always a reason, it is just a case of understanding that reason or explanation for that reason that confuses us and leaves room for a belief to fill the gap. I believe in much of what we currently describe as the paranormal and I do believe there is an explanation, we just don't know or understand it yet. We are constantly on the search for something. We are constantly looking for an explanation and when we can't find it? Well, then it is down to what people choose to believe or not.

It was once believed that if you threw the accused witch into the water you could tell if they were a witch or not. Float, you are a witch, sink and you were not. The outcome was the same, however. One thing it did not prove to anyone was if they were or were not a witch.

Time changes one's understanding of events and the gap in understanding is filled and we move onto the next topic.

As far as the World we speak of as the supernatural, I do believe it is real, just once again not something we fully understand. I do also believe that one day we will. It is because of the lack of available and provable knowledge that leaves room for people to have differing opinions and beliefs on the subject. As time has shown, where there is doubt or lack of proof should I say, there can be a tendency for some to take advantage and play with people's minds and beliefs for their own gain. We shall not do that here. We stand by Sir Arthur and prove it must be the Truth!

Sometimes we see things and think "what was that?" and then sometimes we see things because we want too. When you have a strong belief in a subject then you will more than likely see something that has another explanation than the one you believe to be true.

This is a very common state of affairs when it comes to photographs. Often images can be seen that are more often or not, just shadows and tricks of the light. The camera, even in its advanced form, is still not as good at receiving images as the eye. the human brain can interpret a greater amount of visual information than the camera on your phone! When you have a great belief you can interpret the captured image any way you want. The result is you can see things that are not there or not as they seem to be.

 An orb may very well just be dust or an insect moving in the air, a common problem in photography as it is often too close to the lens for correct focus and results in a blur. Then there is the matter of lens flare. this happens when a light reflects through the glass lenses causing the effect of a bright dot or streak. if you are facing into the light it is very common indeed.

 A picture of a chair may show the pattern of a face, a reflection in a mirror. More often than not they are just that, Patterns and reflections.

 This does not mean all should be debunked. sometimes the image could be the real thing. We have to remember that a photograph is two dimensional and has limited reproduction qualities. They have been one of the biggest tools for deception ever, whether it be

deliberate or otherwise. It has often been said "
The camera never lies" unless we want it too!

When we read a ghost story or horror book we
release adrenaline into our bodies. If we took a
roller coaster or something similar, the same
happens. We have the knowledge that it will
come to an end and we are safe. Sometimes it
is the unbelief in a subject that has more of a
scare factor than actual belief.

We want to believe in something and we tell
ourselves it is real but our subconscious says
differently. All the time a little voice in our
heads is telling us it is not real. We then find
ourselves in a "safe zone" where we can feel
the rush of the adrenaline brought on by the
fight or flight mode. yet be in no need to do
either.

This isn't to say that things don't go bump in
the night, perhaps they do! What it does do is
to give us a safe zone to play in. This is why so
many people see things that have a
reasonable explanation and jump to an
automatic conclusion that it must be
supernatural first and foremost.

People have turned away from the Bible and

other doctrines and turned into ghost hunting shows etc. there is the same amount of evidence for both just as much as there is no solid evidence of either, just what people choose to believe.

   All this said I do believe things go bump in the night but it is a very difficult subject area to work in. With so many moving parts one has to try and see the wood through the trees and that isn't easy. The whole subject can make your head hurt when you try and work towards a conclusion. When television and media get involved there is a pressure on them to entertain and raise viewing numbers unless the producers have very deep pockets, broadcasting is not cheap! What starts out as a genuine idea can soon become tainted or become corrupted. When the need to increase the suspense of an event in order to obtain numbers for viewing, the initial concept and genuine honesty can quickly be tarnished. The need for preservation in the vastly competitive marketplace becomes the number one goal.

   Television broadcasting is big business and not purley to entertain or inform. It is about corporations making money, lots of it. That is when "innocent" events start to happen, like stones or objects being thrown, responsive tappings and the likes. I doubt very much a true believer would walk into a room and antagonize a Demon? Let's be honest, if you believe in Demons then you know they are particularly nasty and have nothing to do with ghosts! They are nothing more than servants of the Devil and then you are into a whole new world of investigation and one would hope you have the training of a priest!

No harm is meant, just the need to boost entertainment value and so keep viewers While the first few times it has a positive effect overall it creates more scepticism and results in loss of true believers and loses respect for the work as a whole. Most investigations into the supernatural tend to be fruitless and dull to the observer. This in itself would then lead to broadcasting what might be of interest to some but not enough to justify the broadcasters, remember they are not interested in the subject, just the numbers. So a few games are thrown in to liven things up. Have you ever watched "Scrooged" with Bill Murray? He wanted to staple antlers to a mouse's head for effect? There were many examples in that film that were a direct attack on the industry.

So why do we believe? Firstly because of the above mentioned and secondly because we may have been involved in our own experiences. We may have accounts from people we trust and know or just too many people have had similar events and experiences of the same thing at the same time or place.

Before we move further into the paranormal or ghost hunting let us consider a couple of important points.

Set your goals and limits. Why do you want to be an investigator? Is it curiosity, just the need to know? Is it something more spiritual like helping spirits cross over to where they should be or is it scientific? If it is scientific, the need for a rational explanation or reason for a phenomena then you are likely to want to go down the road of gadgets. This leads us to the second point as to how much you can comfortably afford to spend on toys. With a basic EMF unit costing around $45 it is easy to see how costs can start to increase. EMF $45, Camera $100, sound recorder $40 already we have spent $185 and haven't even started! All we need to start is our own senses. They come free with each and every one of us.

How scared are you prepared to be? Sounds daft I know but even the toughest of us can get uneasy when mooching around in the dark. We have gone to a haunted location (allegedly) it is dark and the mind starts to play its games. This in itself adds to the fun of the chase because many of us like a good scare for reasons discussed earlier. When things start to trigger your "gut" feelings and anxiety starts to creep in you have probably gone far enough. No matter how silly you may feel pay attention to it and leave. Being on edge is one thing being terrified is another. The basic state of anxiety can soon turn to terror and then panic. Not only can you do yourself some psychological harm but that of others around you. When starting out it should be fun not fear.

It is always a good idea to write your goals and limits down. It will help to record your development in the field and remind you of what you are capable of.

Chapter 2

What is the paranormal?

The definition as supplied by the Merriam Webster dictionary

paranormal adjective

para·nor·mal | \ ˌper-ə-'n□r-məl , ˌpa-rə- ; 'per-

ə-ˌn□r- , 'pa-rə- \

Definition of Paranormal
: not scientifically explainable:
SUPERNATURAL

 I think Ghosts fall into the category of "outside the understanding of science", along with telekinesis and clairvoyance, for now anyways, Once science has discovered how and why these events take place then it will no longer be parallel to the normality of life and understanding as science knows and then we will have to pick a new word. It won't, however, make it any less fantastic. We know how the television works but it is still a fantastic invention even though science knows how it functions and has an explanation. It is no longer seen as outside of the norm. Ghosts, however, are still outside of what science takes as natural and so it is dubbed supernatural.

I personally don't care how science chooses to label it, or if it is explained. It is still a mind-blowing concept to live with!

We have all heard stories and tales that are nothing more than urban myth or legends but how many of us have actually met the people concerned or have encountered them? Be honest, not many. Take the Loch Ness monster for example. So many stories have been told about it. So many tales passed from generation to generation, but have you seen it? Probably not but you have heard of someone who has right? This does not mean that it is an out and out fraud there may very well be a beastie out there, we just don't know. There is the main reason behind so many beliefs, we just don't know.

A sceptic is a person who has doubts about things that other people believe(see Collins

English dictionary) especially religions and the likes. We need them to keep things real. Without them, one could easily fall back into the realms of medieval times and just believe in folk law without any reasoning or doubt. There would never be any progression into research or understanding of a matter. One would just follow the masses and believe anything they are told. This is particularly true were this subject is concerned. There are so many possibilities to think about it is easy for blind belief to get in the way of choosing between fact or fiction.

 I like sceptics, they make you think. What I don't like is the kind that just dismisses something because they just believe differently and don't bother to research something a little further. There are times and issues where it is almost impossible to obtain hard facts or tangible evidence, Christianity for example, and then it does seem to be a case of believing or disbelieving. Whatever works for you. But if one is going to say for or against a specific subject then one should at least make the effort to do a little research!

Chapter 3

The Dark!

Why is it that ghosts only come out to play at night? Ghosts and paranormal activities are there day and night. The day for a ghost is no longer an existence as we know it. We are born, live and die in a period of time that is broken up into day and night. It is divided into hours and minutes and we live it accordingly. A ghost on the other hand is an energy trapped into a specific section of time that overlaps into ours.They do not need to take a nap or go to bed. They just do what they do in accordance to their particular circumstances.

So why do we see them of a night? Why do ghost hunting expeditions and investigations take place of a night?

There are several reasons why and they do

overlap to a degree. It is common for people to experience day time events but it is passed of as something rational. The same event of a night may very well be reported as a supernatural occurrence, yet the event was the same?

In the light of day we are at our busiest. Working, living our lives with all they entail. When the sun goes down for most of us it is when the senses start to relax and we are more susceptible to outside events. Our senses change and our mind starts to view things differently. Perhaps we are tired, or our eyesight starts to wain and lose focus? This would be a common problem for people with short sight. Light entering the eye does not emit quite the right amount of information to the brain and we start to see things. We leave it to the brain to fill in the missing gaps in the information supplied. This can have a double sided effect. We either start to misread what we see and invent something that isn't really there or we allow a higher sense to pick up a different level of vibration.

With a change in our sensitivity and the natural effect of sight being confused by the dark we raise our anxiety and so release adrenaline. "What was that?" was it just a shadow or something else? An image of a ghost like figure is more likely to stand out in dim light than full day light. Ever noticed how the inside of a store or house is difficult to see when it is a sunny day outside yet the store has its lights on? Well, we get a similar effect with the mind when it comes to ghost spotting. We don't look for it during the day when they would be harder to see but we do when it is dark and they are easier to see.

If we then take heightened senses and a common place fear of the dark we have created the perfect environment for ghost watching. Television teams play on this. Not to debunk their authenticity, but from an effect point. If you are already in the right state of mind,their show has a greater impact on the psyche. Your snuggled down with candle light with your favorite snack to hand watching ghosts are us, perfect conditions for the mind to engrose itself with the subject and stand the hairs up on your neck!

Our fear of the dark is there from long ago. Man couldn't see so well after dark and predators would use the dark to their advantage. So we would huddle up and bed down for the night. This inbuilt caution would follow us through generation after generation. All we have done is replace one reason with another. The chances of something or someone attacking us of a night are very small indeed, yet we still need to feed that fear with something, so why not ghost shows?

How do we tell if it is real or imagination? When you are in an a state of alert, that is actually looking for something, then there will almost certainly be some sort of fear attached to your state of mind. That is when the imagination starts to fill gaps in your mind. When you are in an Alpha state, watching TV or reading there is no state of alert or fear. When you then see a shadow in the corner of your eye then your imagination has not produced it. There may very well be a logical explanation but there is also no doubt, you saw something.

What is not assured is how you react to this. Do you shrug it off as nothing, just a shadow, or does your mind go into fight or flight mode? Do you need to find an answer or go back to your book?

From personal experience I have experienced

as much activity of a day as I have of a night. I
used to spend a lot of time working as a reader
and psychic. I found I was at my best during
the day. I would investigate during the day
when my mind was at its clearest. Perhaps I
was just never afraid of the dark so my mindset
was the same day or night, who can say.

 So why do we see ghosts at night? Because
for most of us it is when our brain is in the right
state of relaxation and we are most open to
changes in the world around us.

" OMG! I wonder if humans exist?"

Chapter 4

What is a ghost?

noun

.

an apparition of a dead person that is believed
to appear or become manifest to the living,
typically as a nebulous image.

The word ghost is a synonym for the latin word
spiritus meaning life or breath. It was a word
that was used to describe the human spirit or
life force. The spirit of Christ ie. the holy ghost.
To give up the ghost, give in or admit defeat.
When we look at it from that standpoint what
we have is a reverberation of a past life force
an echo of an energy field if you like. This
would make sense. The entire universe and all
that lives in it is made up of energy. Walls and
trees, rocks and buildings all absorb the energy
that we use and deploy. So why not bounce it
back at us as an echo?

To date there is still no scientific evidence of

ghosts or spectres. This does not mean they don't exist just that there is no hard and fast way of proving either. We also have to ask ourselves if they are the spirits of the dead and can manifest at will and communicate with us (by whatever means) how come there are still unsolved murders? Would a spirit that can communicate with the living be able to say who the bad guy was? If they are just an energy form why do they vary what they do, throw things, make noises. Surely they would just appear to go on doing what they were doing in a repetitive format?

There are many devices out there that can supposedly detect a ghost. Most of them just gadgets with no scientific backing. If the world of physics can't agree on what a ghost is how can we make machines that can detect them? The EMF meter for example is used to measure electrical field fluctuations. Mostly used in medicine, it has become popular with ghost hunters. Where there is a fluctuation in an electrical field then there is likely a ghost. Or is there? No device has to date been used to successfully find a ghost. There could be many reasons for fluctuations in an energy field so it is a bit of a misleading toy that is used when people automatically believe in ghosts and have set their mind on proving it. Still we have no hard and fast evidence they exist or not.

Until science and the world of physics can decide on a definite description we are kind of at a loss as to what we are looking for and determine how it should behave.

If we can't prove an energy force (as of yet) then what is it that we see or hear? There are so many different explanations that for now it boils down to what we each want to believe. What I do know for sure, there is something.

For centuries there have been tales of ghosts and spirits passed down from generation to generation. From the earliest days of mankind stories are passed on and on. Much of our history is buried in folklore and stories. Why would people bother to repeat and pass on tales that had no basis in reality?

What I find sad is the number of frauds and praying mantis that use the field to take advantage of the vulnerable. Those that are in a state of loss and mourning and are easy pickings for the less than scrupulous people of the planet. For those persons I truly hope there is something more!

Chapter 5

Can I play with madness?

One of the main points of the paranormal is the obsession that we can communicate with the afterlife. To be able to contact the deceased is something manind has pondered over for many years. Can we? Many say they can and many more have tried. It was fashionable for ladies to attend after tea seance in America.

The founding of Spiritualism as a religion in the 1800's together with the activities of Mary Todd Lincoln (Wife of president Abraham Lincoln) really brought the whole concept to the public and medias eye in a big way. It became a popular parlour past time and the fraudsters saw their chance of making cash at the hands of the sad and vulnerable.

Harry Houdini soon became one of the most famous of the debunkers of the time. As an expert illusionist he was hard to fool. Hence mediums gained a bad reputation as a result of the fraudsters and parasites that operated offering to contact loved ones and pass on false messages.

One of the biggest "hits" in the field of mediumship is the use of the Ouija board or planchette as it is otherwise known.

Definition of Planchette

a small triangular or heart-shaped board supported on casters at two points and a vertical pencil at a third and believed to produce automatic writing when lightly touched by the fingers.

Variations began to appear into what we now know as the Ouija board. Brought into commercial production in 1890 by Elijah Bond, it was promoted as a parlour game. It became attached to occult use when American occultist Pearl Curran used it as a divining tool during WWI so as to speed up connection with the spirit world. The name Ouija was a patent from the company of Parker brothers who first developed the "game" and were later bought out by Hasbro. Still the name stuck and was used widely by many. The actual word is ancient Egyptian for "good Luck". It was later that William Fuld noticed that the word Ouija was also a combination of both the French and German words for "yes" A far more acceptable way of promoting and marketing the boards, yes yes boards. Mediums during the American civil war would use something similar in seances held for people to contact their loved ones who had died in the war.

The Spirit board or talking board would be laid out showing letters, numbers and in some cases yes or no on it. The idea was to lightly touch the planchette with one finger and request information. A spirit would pick up on the board and guide the pointer or pencil to the answer it wanted to give either by spelling it out or writing the comment.

It is here where things get interesting and the world of science and spiritualism become divided. The idea is simple everybody in the group lightly touches the planchette or glass, the spirit is summoned, uses your energy to help and guide the glass around spelling out words and hey presto, you have an answer. What is common place is for the glass to be pushed and guided by someone at the table living.

They can start the glass of in the right direction and then sit back if they want while the others complete the word. If you think about it you already have the group in the right headspace to start. The mood is right, they have been worked up to it by their own minds and even the sceptical are in a state of curiosity. They can't help it. Once "connection" is established then the minds of the individuals tend to act as one, kind of like a mass hypnosis. Fear starts to rise and all of a sudden the mind no longer focuses on logic and follows along the path in front of it.

There is also the possibility that it might just be real! Many Christian groups and churches frown upon the use of boards. They can open a doorways for bad spirits and even demons to manifest. I have on many occasions been asked to visit a household where the use of a board has gotten out of hand and there is a definite and negative use of the board. Many times it has been a case of their psyche has been affected and the only issue is in fact them. They need to reprogram their thought patterns and come back to earth! There have also been the cases were smudging doesn't help and the services of a priest is required.

There have been many scientific studies and the conclusion is that the board is controlled by the subconscious mind causing muscle movement to direct the board. Something that is actually easy to understand. What is interesting is that they are not sure for definite. A gray area indeed.

  I find it hard to believe that these "games" are
available in regular stores and in most places
available for purchase by anyone 8 years or
older.

  So as it stands in Canada right now, you have
to be 19 to drink, 18 to vote, 17 to drive, 16 for
sex but only 8 to summon demons! I think that
might just be a little mixed up eh? Even if the
whole subject is fake, one should study all the
aspects before using one. Whether it is a
manifestation of the mind or that of a spirit,
you should know what you are doing. If it is
possible to summon demons, which I do by the
way, then this is the perfect portal they require.

  It might be hocus pocus or it might be
genuine, there is no evidence either way. What
is for sure they can mess with your mind and in
some cases bring on a little madness.

Chapter 6

Mediums

Oxford English dictionary
Noun

The intervening substance through which sensory impressions are conveyed or physical forces are transmitted.

One of the most controversial sectors of the whole paranormal world. Mediums. A spiritual medium is in its simplest form a person who acts as a middle man between this world and the realm of the dead. A person who can link both worlds and pass messages back and forth. Depending upon how you see it, it can either be a gift or a curse! Imagine how it must feel to have dead people talking to you and wanting you to pass on the information like it was an everyday event for you? Just imagine, "Hey can you just tell Pam I am here!" What? Erm, not really weird eh?

For most the ability starts to appear when they
are young and know nothing to the contrary.
Everyone can do it, or so they think. Then as
they grow older they tend to hide it from others
because they know it is not the standard for
people to be able to perform this function.
What has a tendency to happen is they start to
think of themselves as abnormal or "strange".
They then start to take on a persona that fits
the image of being different and start to act in
ways that may be considered odd to many.
Their clothing, household decor, view of the
world and most importantly how they interact
with others. Some will learn to control the
ability, others may not. Some want the "gift"
others don't. Whether you are Christian or not,
it will be seen as a gift or a curse. I don't know
of any one who stands in the middle, shrugs
their shoulders and says " it is what it is". I am
sure they do exist, I am just saying I have
never met such a person.

The human race has always had a fascination
with the dead and the after life. Take the cave
paintings in Australia which date back over 28
thousand years! The practice is associated
with several religious-belief systems such as
Vodun, Spiritualism, Spiritism, Candomblé,

Voodoo, Umbanda and some New Age groups. I think it is safe to say that there is something to it! With the onset of a spiritual rising in the USA mediumship most definitely came to the public eye. With President Lincoln's wife leading the charge group seances on spirit readings became a popular pastime of those who had money. Where there is cash there is fraud. It is exactly that which caused a greater public interest in the occupation of mediumship.

The unscruplious fraudster saw a chance to make money. They would, in the guise of a medium, offer their services and con people out of their cash. They would use the aid of accomplices during seances and even go as far as to use the same tricks as an illusionist to falsify the apparition of a spirit! Cardboard cutouts, people knocking on tables and walls. What ever trick that could be used was used. This brought about the onset of the debunkers like Houdini. Top illusionists would spot the tricks quickly and with ease, after all they invented them.

Modern spiritualists and psychics keep very detailed files on their clients or as detailed as they can get. Information like this can be very valuable and are often sold or traded from one medium or psychic to another. If a medium can't obtain personal details of a client (drivers licence, private detective etc.) there's still a very powerful technique that they can use that will allow the psychic to convince people that the psychic knows all about them, their problems, and their deep personal secrets, fears, and desires.

The technique is called cold reading and is probably as old as charlatanism itself... If a medium really could communicate with the dead,would it not be a trivial matter to prove it? All that would be necessary would be for him to do would be to contact any of the thousands of missing persons who are presumed dead and correctly report where the body is. Of course, this is never done. All we get, instead, are platitudes to the effect that dear Mildred who loved dogs is happy on the other side and to tell you she is doing fine. Have you noticed how many are actually asking questions? It may be something simple like they sense purple, who is it that likes the colour purple? So you answer and all of a sudden, they have information to build on. Was it important, who likes it and so on. Then you find you have given all the information they require to deliver what appears to be a connection. All the time you made it for them.

 This in itself does not mean there is no truth in the ability some people may have in bridging the gap. What it does do is cast doubt over the subject completely. I don't imagine the act of contacting the dead and passing messages backwards and forwards is an easy thing to do. It isn't as though you can just send a text from your iphone(well not yet!) so I can only imagine messages to be difficult to understand. The languages of the day for example. Many would say that spirits have a way of understanding and communicating no matter what language or words are used. What a convenient answer. It is a bit like saying God works in mysterious ways! You either believe it or you don't. This is why genuine readers and mediums may have a difficult time translating a message or have a little vagueness around an answer. Most of the time I am sure they are just confused by what they encounter and yet are under pressure to deliver for the client. There will always be that push to impress especially if they charge for their services.

 I do not know of anyone who can proclaim to be an expert in this field, how can they? So

many different opinions and yet no evidence
that it is real in the first place. How can anyone
say they know for sure when as a race, who
puts man on the moon, can't even prove that
such an ability or discipline exists!

 We have to judge by our own experiences and
make our choices accordingly. If we employ an
"expert" then a case of buyer beware arises.
Simply put, pays your money take your
chances!.

Chapter 7

Things that go bump in the night.

There are many places in the world that are known for their notoriety as haunted. People have reported a vast array of spooky goings on that have no apparent logical explanations. Pubs, churches, abandoned psychiatric hospitals to name a few. Many locations stand out as being just perfect for apparitions and paranormal events. Where there has been an abundance of human action there is bound to be an appropriate energy reaction. So when we think of a Church graveyard or notorious prison, we automatically accept there would be paranormal activity.

What is of greater interest is the kind of event that takes place when there is no apparent reason. You live in a new house in a suburb then one night something odd happens? You can't explain it, it just does out of the blue. If the home has just been constructed on reclaimed land one could associate the event with what was formerly there. An old monastery or hospital. Perhaps an old school or poor house or even the sight of a horrific murder! What if there was none of that? Just new homes built on virgin land that used to be just a field? Grass, cows or maybe even a tree or two. Then one has to think how do spirits attach? What makes them appear? When we enter this point of thought it is time to reach for the aspirin! When we don't have any certain evidence or proof of the existence of such things then how can we explain their behavior? Yet it happens and there are many people who would give many different causes and explanations.

I once worked with a group of readers and mediums who all reached the agreement that sometimes spirits are just passing through. They are souls on a journey that just so happens to take them through your property and hence appear in your world. If this is the case then why would they stop and take interest in the new surroundings? After all they are just spirits doing what they were doing at the time of their existence. For them to stop and investigate means that they are aware of their surroundings and have some form of cognitive capability. A whole new perspective is formed. The existence of an afterlife. A life with its own rules and interactions, not just a replay of energies that have been released back into our time and world.

 We need to address what has happened and how it interacted with the person. Did it just appear and go about whatever it was doing or did it actually interact in some way? Did something get moved? An item misplaced? Did something of a more serious nature take place? Where you threatened in some way or did you just feel threatened by its presence? If you were to feel just threatened or uncomfortable by its presence, then you can assume it is just passing through and is a release of energy that means no harm. How could it cause harm? It is just an echo of times gone by. If however there is direct interaction we have a whole new way of looking at it.

 It is here that we start to get involved in more than just ghosts. We are getting into the concept of spirituality as a religious format. We can no longer follow the pretence that they are just echos of past events but they are of a realm attached to ours, but based in a different time scale a parallel existence. The soul has moved on from the living person as we know them and onto the next stage of their journey. If a soul or spirit is trapped somewhere between this world and the next, has some form of cognitive understanding and function, then we can expect interaction. They may be confused by events, have unfinished business, or maybe just too scared to move on and complete their journey.

When the energies from one dimension start to interact with those of another, there are no guidelines as to what may happen. Physicists are only just getting to terms with what is going with our world let alone the possibility of a parallel universe! I am sure if Doctor Who was available for comment we could get a clearer understanding of events and how they interact but at the last check he was busy making a TV show and wasn't able to comment. Apart from that option I can only think of chatting to God about it, but there again I think he may be busy and otherwise occupied! This kind of leaves it to ourselves to work out and why we can't have expert proof one way or another. While believers say they know for sure science will say differently, a bit like the bible in a way. Either you do or you don't. make your own choice because no one can prove it either way.

 We have looked at why there are more supernatural events of a night as opposed to day. What is a natural effect s that when something does happen of a night it's fear factor and sensation provoking aspects are greater. When we have daylight it is easier to feel more relaxed and likely to look for an obvious explanation. When it is dark our self preservation mode is on higher alert. This is due primarily to our genetic inbuilt laws on survival.

 We are at our most vulnerable in the dark because vision is limited, so when something does go bump our mind starts to make assumptions to fill in the gaps we can't see. Our imagination starts to kick in and the obvious is overlooked as a result. This does not mean something strange and outside of an ordinary state of affairs is happening, it might well be. What it does effect is our sense of reason and it becomes more difficult to separate fact from fiction so as to speak.

 How can we make a judgment based on only a glimpse of a picture? Well that is the million dollar question, yet our bodies and minds have

to make it there and then. We have to make a
call one way or another. Fight or flight.

When I was a young boy (5 or 6) I remember
standing with my brothers, well two of them,
and a couple of their friends in the kitchen. It
was a newly built house on a very small estate
in what was then just farm land. We were a bus
ride from any sort of town centre os shopping
areas. While listening in on the conversations
of the older members of the group I noticed in
the corner of my eye an arm hanging over the
open kitchen door. It scared me to the point
where I let out an involuntary yelp. My elder
brother ran into the kitchen to see what was
happening and I explained what I saw. Both he
and the others began a search of the kitchen
and house and could find no one else who may
have played a prank on a young kid.

The interesting thing was the door opened
inwards and up against the wall behind it.
There was no room for anyone to hide! The
overall conclusion was that it had been a trick
of the light. I was happy with this decision as
grown up kids had made it. Until my father
came home and announced that a work mate
had lost his arm in an accident!

This event had two affects on me. One was I
psychic? and secondly why had it appeared
here? I will never know. The grown up kids still
called it a trick of the light and just coincidence
but it did start my curiosity into the subject. It
took several years before I developed my
interests but the seed had been sown.

Even now I can still recall the event with great
clarity, knowing that it was no trick of the light,
but what was it? Perhaps it was some form of
premonition or clairvoyance? It was only after a
few years I discovered t was a friend of my
fathers and he actually had visited a few times
and lived close by. Had some form of spirit
tried to tell of his misfortune? He was still alive
so it could not be him so if not him then what
was going on? I never discovered an answer
that satisfied my curiosity but instead just made
it grow.

I used to attend a local church as a young
man and had become a friend of the Vicar
(Cannon to be exact) and asked him one
Sunday night after service what his take on
ghosts would be? I was surprised that he didn't
just dismiss it as anti-christian mumbo jumbo
as I was expecting. His outlook on the matter
was that they were the souls of the dead that

had not made the journey to heaven. They had somehow become stuck in the divide between here and there and where in fact lost and confused. He likened it to the signals at a switchboard and when passing the line over the connection wasn't solid and the transfer was left incomplete. In Fact it would reverberate onto other lines causing the voices to appear on another persons line, or crossed wires as they would call it. He did not believe however, that mediums and the likes could be temporarily play host to a spirit in order to communicate with the living nor did he believe in crystal balls or fairground gypsies. He just saw it as a transfer of the soul that had gotten messed up. So now I had my own experience and the word of a holy man to draw on, I was convinced on something, I just wasn't sure what?

 Just a little something extra on the church where I went. Strangely enough a pub had been built right next door to it. It probably took thirty seconds to walk from the church to the bar. Finish church on a Sunday night, hop to the pub with its olde world charm and log fire, have a beer with the Vicar and relax in its warmth. Something that I would do with my girlfriend every week end. Every Sunday we would have a few drinks then venture out into the night and wait for our bus at the stop right outside the front of the church.

 The church had originally been built in the 1100's and was actually listed in the Doomsday book. While waiting at the stop we would watch old George, who would wander past on his way home to a small house seemingly not far away. He looked in his late 80's and always wore the same trench coat that he had kept from his days as a fighter pilot in the Royal Air Force. His name and wings clearly visible, he seemed to wear it with pride. He would stumble past and we always nodded and said hello, he never replied or acknowledged the greeting, just kept walking. It was 1979 and I was 18 years of age. When mentioning this to the bar server in casual conversation I was told George had died in 1976! He had fought in the Battle of Britain and had lost the will to live after his wife of fifty years died from cancer. He had survived her by 12 months.

 One thing that I had become to realize was that one only seemed to see or encounter a ghost when one was least expecting it or realising it. To go and search for an apparition did not work out. There was never any event to record. Things would only happen when you were least likely to expect it like bumps in the night. You are focused on your life, getting on with day to day living.

Your attention is not focused on the potential experience of other worldly happenings. That is when you are most likely to have an experience. I am not talking of experienced or seasoned ghost hunters, I am talking about the everyday person.

Let us first dismiss what the likely cause of a noise is. During the day there tends to be a lot more noise and distraction taking place. Maybe the dishwasher is running or the television is on. Are there children playing or someone nearby doing renovations? These and many other events hide and distract from all kinds of normal noises that start to appear later in the evening when things calm down. The children go to bed, the dishes are done it is time to relax a little before heading to bed yourselves. You eventually call it a day and head off to brush your peggies and turn in. The lights are off and it is nigh night world.

The quiet of the night allows for what seems

an amplification of any sound. When you are in the state between being awake and asleep the mind is starting to file away the events of the day and get on with its routine of refresh and try and fix the effects of strain on our bodies. Then you hear a noise and it brings you back into consciousness. Was it a noise you haven't heard before? Chances are you have but just didn't pay it any thought or attention. You were probably to busy doing other things to notice or care.

When everybody in the neighborhood is awake and doing their business sounds become confused or overlooked. Water pressure is lower as a direct result of families doing their dishes and bathing all around the sametime. When the pressure running through pipes is lower than during the day then they have a tendency not to vibrate as much. When the pressure is higher the strain on the pipe is greater and the chances of knocking and vibrating is higher. A leaking faucet or leak will become more pronounced and create a greater level of noise when there is higher pressure. Is there an air bubble in the central heating units making a sound? There is a good chance you didn't notice while there were other sounds being made. Take a sound you haven't noticed before and add in the disorientation of being almost asleep and you have the potential for the mind to become confused and jump to the wrong conclusion.

Do you live in a rural area? I know I do. In fact, the middle of nowhere to be honest. I live on Vancouver island 15 mile from any form of town or city. There are 16 houses on the estate all with ½ to 5 acres each, lots of trees and no street lights. The area is on the edge of a rainforest and it is not uncommon to find a black bear in your garden! Very often we have racoons stealthily crossing the roof of the house. In fact when I say stealthily I mean as about as sneaky as an elephant with clogs on! We have rats, bears, deer, opossums you name it. Cougars and rabbits, it is quite a zoo. Trust me there is nothing quite like deer slowly munching on grass outside your window of a night to make you ask "what on earth?"

How about you live in a densely populated area where the houses are close together or joined even? Was that something the neighbor did? Was it a passer by in the street? When we take into account all the probable causes then what is left is there for investigation.

Do you see faces in the walls and such?

It is only when you have removed or analyzed
all the possible rational explanations that you
can start to think about paranormal activity. I
have a friend who was concerned about a bag
of his late father's clothes moving of a night. It
never happened during the day just of a night.
He inspected the bag on several occasions
and found nothing. That night he saw it move
again, this time he rose from his bed and
decided to investigate. As he drew closer to the

bag the movement stopped. He opened the
bag shining his flashlight and there was the
answer, a mommy mouse and her babies.
They had crept in during the night to bed down.
Little buggers!

When it has been warm of a day the cool night
air will result in timbers contracting this too can
cause noises in the night. We are used to
ehses events and can often tell what is going
on. The young child may not understand and
will be, perhaps,a little scared of the sound.
The grown ups won't be, unless they are on

their own and the imagination takes over. The fear raised by sounds is all relative to the age and state of mind of the individual.

 Watch a horror movie on your own in the dark and the plumbing goes crack, the result is you jump out of your skin! You have created the correct conditions for your senses to be on edge. It is when you are just walking down the length of the house or sitting quietly in your chair and you hear a strange sound, that is when it is time to investigate. If it is a paranormal event then the chances are the sounds will continue right up the point when you are almost on top of it or something else causes a distraction, like a light being switched on.

 We have discussed why ghosts are more likely to appear in the dark so why would switching on a light cause their disappearance? When you turn a light on you complete a circuit and an energy charge is released lighting the bulb. This sudden burst of energy can be all that is needed to refocus all other energies that may be around. After all if we have fight or flight senses why shouldn't a ghost? They are after all just another format of us.

Sefton Church England.

This Norman built building was erected in 1291. The original land was consecrated in 1170 as a private chapel for the Molyneux family.

Chapter 8

Where do we find ghosts?

Here we have the "Million dollar" question, where do we find ghosts? Answer: anywhere. If we are to assume that they are an entity caught between worlds then why would they be in just one particular sort of place place? If the spirit is attached to a place or item or they died with unfinished business then one would be correct for going where the story of their demise leads us. If, however, it was just confused by events and missed the opportunity to pass on at the designated time then it could well be lost and roaming so it could appear anywhere.

A busy location that is old and seen a lot of human (or Animal) activity is a good place to start. Why an old house as opposed to a new one? Because there has been a lot more energy omitted during its history. The longer we go back in time the more violence and reckless behaviour there was amongst people. This in itself would lead to a greater chance of a ghost developing. There is a greater chance of confusion in people. Why had they been attacked or murdered?

Health care was limited and there was more exposure to uncontrolled disease. Mental health issues were most definitely poorly handled. With unacceptable conditions, the sick and mentally unwell were left in disgusting conditions and would die as a result. There is no such thing as a pleasant death. All death is unpleasant but to die in conditions not fit for a sewer rat makes it all the more unpleasant. Naturally this would have led to extreme confusion in the subjects concerned.

Conditions in poor houses, hospitals and mental institutions were to say the least bad. It was easy to overlook conditions and turn a blind eye to events that took place. As far as the general population of a country were concerned, they didn't exist. That is not to say there were no persons concerned and trying to change things, there were. Just not enough at the time. We were left with the perfect conditions for lost and confused souls to form. Conditions in factories, military bases, households and street people were all poor. Unless you had money you were nothing of any importance to the world.

Similar conditions and events were common place around the globe. The actions of man against fellow man is one of intolerable acceptance, yet, it took place and still does.

So where do we look for ghosts? Wherever mankind has lived or worked. There is no set place or venue.

If we are looking for a venue with more certainty of spooky residents then there is a short list of favorites. Old or abandoned hospitals (including mental institutions), churches and monasteries. Life as a monk was not all that people think. Disease and poor conditions took their toll just like any other place. Just because it was a monastery did not protect it or make it exempt from the forces of nature in any way.

One of the best places to start hunting would be somewhere old and steeped in history. Stay away from tourist ghost hunts and walks. While they do inform you of the history and paranormal events, they are designed to entertain and make money. If you have to pay to investigate paranormal activity then there is likely to be no fruitful outcome! They do however give you a great idea of where to start when less busy. They also provide useful background information as well as provide good entertainment. I have been on a few, they are immense fun and I would do it again, just not to investigate seriously.

 I have here some accounts of private encounters that have been sent to me. Out of respect for individuals requests, names have been changed but the events are verbatim.

Canterbury Cathedral England.
Karen Becconsall

" In the tunnels just before you go into where Thomas Becket was murdered, by having the top of his head cut off!, is the location of where a young woman was strangled. She was left in the passageway for dead. You can feel her presence as she appears to still walk in confusion and there is, as felt by many, a definite drop in temperature as she passes by. As you make your way to exit the Cathedral at the far end of there are several stained glass windows where you can often see a man dressed in shakespearean type clothing complete with the ruffled neck collar I saw him during daylight! Along with others in the group I was with!"

Thomas Becket was the Archbishop and was murdered in 1170.

An encounter in the UK.
Jackie Trent

"My husband was away on business and my daughter was upstairs when my very placid dog who began barking and fussing at the corner in the corner of the room on the ceiling. I calmed her down and she settled. About 30-60 mins later I received a phone call to say that my husband had had an out of hospital cardiac arrest. He had been resuscitated at the scene and taken to hospital and undergone Coronary Angiogram and had a further event. He never regained consciousness."

Is it possible that he had an out of body experience and came to say goodbye? With all the energy in a trauma room there would be a heightened chance of spirit activity. As there is no definite conclusion as to what happens to the spirit upon death who can give a definite answer? Why would it project itself to the ceiling in the corner of the room? Could it be that the dog picked up on the energy from that direction as opposed to the room itself?

If you want to find a ghost then use your dog. They seem to have an uncanny way to spot these things. They are without doubt far more sensitive than people. Once again we can't know for sure just exactly what they sense. We know they have increased powers of detection, smell and hearing but to what extent? Have you noticed just how they know your sick or unhappy even when you don't show it? Makes you wonder just how much we do know for sure.

Many of the popular sights are found in areas with deep historical attachments and are of course populated by many visitors hoping to see a ghost or two. Many other sights are reasonably unknown due to the fact that the people involved with sightings or experiences of some form want to keep it quiet. They do not wish to have their name associated to events due to the continuing stigma that they must be whacho for repeating tales of a paranormal nature. Even though we live in more enlightened times such stigmas still exist.

Chapter 9

What tools to use?

Emf meters, Evp meters, spirit boards and on and on. There are so many gizmos available that you could spend a small fortune on gear and still have no results to shout about. We shall take a look at what is needed to get a good start on your investigation bag.

1. Carry case
2. Your senses
3. Notebook and pen
4. Flashlight
5. Camera
6. Sound recorder
7. Spares!

Firstly you need a bag to carry your goodies. Obvious one but so often not thought through. It has to be waterproof or as close as you can get it. Be easy to carry, a shoulder strap helps. I use an old camera case from back in the days

when I worked as a photographer. It is made of
aluminium and padded with foam. The reason
for its use? I already had it! It was designed to
hold 3 Nikon F3 cameras, extra film, a couple
of lenses and flash guns. Now it holds my toys!

 A perfect case would be a backpack. The type
used by hunters and outdoor people. Simple,
rugged and pretty much waterproof. They do
not have to be expensive to start. Watch out for
military surplus or car boot sales (garage
sales) you will be surprised as to where these
things turn up. Another useful item would be a
utility vest. The type used by fishermen or
military persons. They have plenty of pockets
and are designed to hold your good securely
but allowing ease of access.

  The most basic tools required you already
have. Eyes, ears and sense of smell. These
are probably the most useful tools you can
possess. All the electrical goods, cameras and
sound recording equipment is fine but
ultimately it is your own senses that matter
most. The human eye can collect more
information than any camera. The only
cameras that would sense something different
would be the specialist type for infrared or heat
signatures. Even with these there is still no

definite way to prove or disprove a sighting.

I find that a notebook and pen to be the next on my list of must haves. It allows you to record events and your feelings. It is also there if you want to try your hand at automatic writing. A technique used by psychics and investigators alike. A very useful tool indeed. Just remember pocket size is best!

When it comes to flashlights there are two types that would be useful. The standard handheld so you can easily see where you are going and the headband type. I prefer these so that I can keep my hands free but they are not so easily turned on and off like a hand held. Also if I decide to use a Gopro type camera even my head isn't big enough for both! So I carry both types. When it comes to choosing your flashlight get the best you can afford. You will be surprised at how much of a battering they will take out in the field.

A simple digital camera that can take videos as well as stills is probably a must. If it has night vision as well even better. It does not have to be a state of the art device. Just one that will record in high definition and have some capability to record sound as well. I use a cyber shot by Sony. It is waterproof to 10m and gives an image that is perfectly good for downloading to my computer. Again it is an item that I was already in possession of. You don't have to spend a fortune on a fancy camera at this stage if ever. You are starting out so why blow a small fortune on gear if you might not even like the pastime? Cold, wet and scary? Give it a go first it is not for everyone.

 The last thing I would pack starting out is spares! Batteries and bulbs have a habit of failing in areas of high paranormal activity. No one can really explain this phenomenon, it just happens so be ready. Some believe it is an entity drawing energy so as to communicate, this I doubt. Others believe it is disruption in electromagnetic fields that cause the drain. A more likely conclusion but who knows for sure?

Chapter 10

Research

One of the most important things anyone involved with ghost hunting can do is research. It would be easy to sit in the cold dark damp of a church yard only to find nothing happens. Your mates are all down the bar in the warmth and you are out in the cold. Two things can happen here. 1. You lose your enthusiasm or 2. get cold! When you consider that on average only one vigil produces an experience of some sort out of every four a bit of research could have saved you a lot of time and effort.

What are we looking for with our research? The answer is an increased chance of finding something. The main thing about ghost hunting is that there is no definite proof of where to find them or, if, they really exist. That is the whole point of the project you have undertaken. To find proof either for or against. Yes it can be about having fun and doing something a little different with your time which is no bad thing. I have known many people involved with paranormal investigating that do it just to be involved in a social group and have an interest in a hobby like format. Regular meetings, social interaction and ultimately friendships with like minded people. It is all good. The discovery of something new is always interesting and when you have others to share it with even better. This does not however change the fact that the search for evidence is foremost.

When we say research what are we looking for? Firstly we are looking for a place that has a reputation for activity. Is it known for its spooky goings on? Rather than just descend on a place on the off chance it may be haunted. We need something to go on. We are looking for stories and some sort of evidence to start with. The internet is a useful tool in these matters as well as local libraries.

First we find the location we are interested in, a building, a church yard or even a highway! Where I currently live the main road through the little town centre was haunted by an apparition of a white lady. She would appear to motorists by the side of the road in the form of a cloudy white spectre. She was said to have no arms or legs and a hideous face.It was said that she died in a First Nations battle. When road crews discovered the skeleton while making road improvements the hauntings stopped. By taking time to research and trace the history of a location we improve our chances and do not waste time. Who would have thought the side of a road would be the home of a ghost?

Did the location you were thinking about have a powerful history? Ask yourself what sort of people lived there, why and when. Was there a reason for them to be dissatisfied with life? Poor living conditions and health issues played apart in the lives of many in years gone by. Indigenous peoples all across the world have been subjected to cruelty and harsh conditions. Does the site you are looking at fall into this area?

Many locations have been changed over the years with development and expansions. This does not mean that any activity has been removed it may still be there it's just the site that has changed. It is very common to hear on ghost hunting shows and on ghost tours how things have changed. It often sounds like 'and on this site in…." or "the previous site.." This is why apparitions often seem to be floating or legless they are operating and appearing on a different plain or level as to what is there today. Perhaps a new floor or extension or maybe the new building is actually lower than the previous one. In the 18 and 1900's it was common to build houses on stilts so as to be above the street where sewerage was just dumped. It was common practice in london during the reign of Elizabeth 1st to empty dirty dish water and toilet pans out of the window and onto the street below.

 Another good source of records is the church especially old ones. Records of births and deaths give a good background to an area. Who lived there and when. The records will often include details of parents and how they came to be there. While one may not be a follower of god, one can't deny their ability to keep records, they are second to none for accuracy.

 Even if you know a site has a good reputation for happenings it does not hurt to do a little digging beforehand so that you have an idea of who or what you are looking for.

This kind of information can be extremely useful when hunting ghosts and can be easily obtained. It is well worth the time. You get a history lesson and aid in locating where you need to be. No more wasted time sitting under a damp bridge while your mates are in the pub!

Another way to find out information is to contact a guided ghost tour operation. Let them know you want a genuine hunt and not just the tourist type. Many operations will be able to suggest a good tour for you and these make an excellent place to start. While their main goal is to entertain the tourist who is paying to be entertained they did not start out thus. Commercial tours have mostly been developed from genuine ghost hunts. For many operators that is where their true passion lies but they need to make money! I don't think I have come across many who won't oblige you though a dare say, they are in existence today.

When you decided on a location see if you can find blueprints or old map of the area. This together with tales and stories can help narrow down your field of search. You are not only becoming a researcher here but a bit of an historian also. Your interest has gone from just finding a ghost to finding out the history of the people and places. Cool eh?

A headstone can provide you with useful
information on the people who lived and died in an
area. Some are very basic others carry detail on
how they died.

Chapter 11

Can a ghost hurt you?

This all depends on what you mean by hurt you. If you mean apparate, pick up a shovel and the bang you on the head with it then very probably not. There have been accounts of light body damage, scratches and blotches, there have also been accounts of other bodily manifestations.

It is widely believed that many marks are self inflicted or manifested but we can't say for sure. I have not as of yet met anybody with anything more. This does not mean to say it hasn't happened, just that I have never encountered anyone who has been assaulted. For that matter, I have never met anyone who knows someone were it has been evident. I have heard tales and urban myths, just never encountered it first hand.

If you mean hurt mentally, then yes. Due to the nature of an investigation there is an increased chance of psychological vulnerability. The overall state of mind is alerted by the whole stage of what you are entering into. Something at the back of your mind is telling you to be afraid while another part of your mind is saying you are safe. This split in mental focus can cause a slight state of self hypnosis and render you vulnerable psychic attack.

It is important on all investigations to be aware of your surroundings and how you are feeling. It is hard to say if you are being attacked by an outside force or you are attacking yourself mentally. Either way you need to able to protect yourself.

The best protection you can afford yourself is to stay alert. A strong and controlled mind is all it needs even in the presence of a spirit. The only way that they can control you is if you let them! When ghost hunting it is not an occupation you do alone in the first place. Remember the old adage "There is safety in numbers". If you believe you are under attack then simply excuse yourself from the location. There is no point in risking your sanity for the sake of keeping face. No one will think any the less of you. In fact it would be a sensible and noteworthy thing to do. You can always return to a venue but you can't always return from madness.

There are many books and blogs written about psychic protection how about physical protection? When we are walking about we do not tend to think about where we put our feet. It is normal to be walking on solid ground and tendered pavements. When we enter a room that has a slippery surface, spilled water for example, then there tends to be warning signs or if it has been raining our onboard computer(the brain) automatically accounts for it.

What happens when we walk around looking for ghosts? The senses are changed with natural apprehension at the environment around us and as to what we might encounter. We do not adjust for awkward flooring and changes in ground texture. We are focused on other things and there is the danger of stumbling. It is often difficult to walk on uneven surfaces at the best of times but when your conscious mind is focusing on finding ghosts then attention to your footing takes second place. Wear strong anti slip footwear!

High heels are great for looking good in the workplace or social event but they are not of much use on a ghost hunt. (What if you have to run!) the tapping sound made from heels or solid sole shoes will not upset a ghost but it will distract yourself and others in the group. Remember you are trying to hear strange sounds and there can be nothing better than the pitter patter of shoes.

The sound of footsteps is one of the sounds you will be listening out for so we don't need the distraction of yours or someone else's. Imagine the disappointment of slowly tracking footsteps only to round a corner and find it is your buddies feet. Many locations will have uneven floors, abandoned buildings may very well have fallen debris to contend with, so protect your feet. A fall in the dark could very well injure you and also bring the nights adventures to an abrupt halt. A pair of good quality runners (no pun intended!) would be ideal and they are not going to kill your budget. I use my hunting boots, yes they were expensive, but I use them a lot when hunting in the woods and mountains so they were worth the expenditure.

If you know the venue you are going to visit has the potential for falling debris then perhaps head protection would be a good idea? A hat or cap works as well as a toque (beanie hat) you want to eliminate cuts to your head if you need the protection of a hard hat then perhaps you shouldn't be there!

The sort of place where it would be advisable and can very often be on your list of venues are caves. Caves were often used by Witches and soothsayers and there are plenty to be investigated in Europe. Derbyshire, England for example, has many pin hole caves used by Witches as do many of the other counties there. Due to the nature of caves a hard hat would be advisable to protect your head from stalactites and loose rocks. Many caves have been developed into show caves with paving and lights but for the more adventurous there are plenty of smaller caves to be found.

One item of safety that is inexpensive to buy and extremely useful is a safety vest. A luminous vest like the sort used by road work staff and miners for example, can really be of value when out stumbling around in the dark. They can be obtained at most hardware stores and even online.

Wet weather gear is a difficult one. Many items designed to keep the water out are not designed to be silent unless you are prepared to splash out on the more expensive items intended for hikers and campers. I tend to wear my hunting garments. They are soft, silent and waterproof. Due to the nature of hunting they need to be as silent as possible yet keep you warm and dry. You wouldn't last long in temperatures of -20c in a regular hoodie! It is up to you how much or what you invest in. if you are an active outdoors type you would probably have more use for these things than if you just want to stay dry on a ghost hunt. I would suggest a bag of spare dry clothes in the car. Wool has a tendency to keep you warm even when wet, denim does not. Something to keep in mind when selecting your gear.

So can a ghost hurt you? Well if you are not mentally ready or kitted out properly then yes. you are ready and dressed for the occasion then extremely unlikely. The most likely effect is to be on your mental state. If you are ready for it, no worries, abovall listen to your "gut" feelings they are the best protection systems you can get.

One thing you must not do is take home an object or souvenir of the night no matter how harmless it may seem. While it may be a case that spirits have difficulty in attaching to strangers not so an object that has been lying around for some time. Even garbage can attract negative attention so it is best not to take chances. The ability to deal with spirits and paranormal events will develop with time and learning. If you think the ghost says "get out!" then do so unless your are of a more advanced capability.

One item that should be in every ghost hunting kit is a carbon dioxide meter. This isn't because ghost emit CO2 it is because it can build up in old buildings. In a poorly ventilated room the buildup of CO2 can cause nausea and fainting amongst investigators. Often believed that it was the suffocating presence it is no more than a build up of scent free, flavor free gas that goes undetected by the senses of a human.

Coal Miners would keep canaries in cages underground for this very reason. The birds would detect the gas buildup and warn the miners letting them make an advanced escape of a harmful situation. The modern day ghost

hunter can be all too quick to find a
supernatural cause and not pay attention to the
obvious. A canary in a cage is not acceptable!
Not only is it cruel to the bird but is noisy and
distracting as well. So we use a meter to check
levels and so avoiding illness.

It is extremely scarce to find record of anyone
being seriously injured by a ghost or even a
poltergeist manifestation. Any injury is like to
be as a result of accident or carelessness. It
has been known for a spirit to appear and
cause a person to trip or stumble but this tends
to be as a result of surprise not actual intent.

When it comes to Demonic evidence then that
is a different thing altogether! Demonic
possession is something of a spiritual matter
and should not be confronted by an
investigator. Leave and set up a face to face
meeting with a minister or priest. The clergy
has spent a lot of years researching and
training for such activity and they are the ones
to deal with it..

DON'T take chances with your health or state
of mind, or anyone else's for that matter, It is
not worth it. Let the professionals do their job.

Demons should be handled by trained professionals. Remember you are entering the world of spiritual matters here and it is best left to the clergy to decide a course of action.

Chapter 12

Useful stuff to know

We have looked at and talked about several aspects of spook hunting. Let us now take a look some general good to know information.

Carry a compass, why? For one they help you keep track of direction when exploring a foreign place (Doh!) but secondly they can spin out of control when there is a disturbance in an electromagnetic field! Whilst surrounding metallic rich objects can cause this, stone in a cave for example, they provide a backup to battery operated devices. Batteries have an uncanny habit of draining quickly in paranormal areas.

Bug spray is another item one should be aware of. When it comes to encounters of the paranormal kind bug spray is of no use whatsoever, but during the summer it can be more than useful in a church yard. Nothing quite like a bug bite to distract you!

"NO! Bug be gone!!"

White chalk is also a good idea. You can mark areas as to where you have been especially in tunnels or caves. If your sense of direction is less than perfect it can help reduce a lot of stress. It is also easily removed and is unlikely to cause any permanent damage to a location. I like to keep a small first aid kit handy, not just in the truck, but a small kit on my person. It is very easy to sustain minor injuries when on a hunt in the dark. A small cut could ruin your adventure and could so easily be fixed with a band aid.

Know who is in your group. Are they chatty and like to talk a lot? This can often be a sign of nerves it could also be they are a chatty person. If it is nervousness then you may want to address it early on in the evening and reassure them they are safe. If someone is not settling down and seems to be getting worse you may need to ask them to leave or partner them up with an experienced hunter who does not seemed perturbed by their chatter. As a former scuba instructor I would often observe people get nervous and then settle or buck it! A frightened person can be a hazard if they decided to bolt on a hunt in the dark. Trip hazards are not easily seen and can result in bad cuts or broken bones.

Are they an introvert? They may be the type of person who likes to quietly observe and take in their surroundings or, it could again be nerves. Keep your eyes open. It is important to know who is in your group so that you can match pairs in accordance to their experience and nervous state. You want the night to be constructive and fun! Who wants to be in any sort of society that isn't fun?

I have mentioned this before and I will say it again. Never go on your own. No matter how brave you are a single mind is always going to be vulnerable to itself or external forces. A companion helps keep you grounded. Simple chit chat makes all the difference and keeps your mind calm. Even if you find on the way home you have forgotten something take a companion with you.

I, like many other hunters, carry a small item of a personal nature, a bit like a good luck charm, that I know is grounded in the world of the living. Many investigators will carry something. Perhaps they may carry a stone or a crucifix. I have known one guy who always carried a fishing fly made out of ravens feathers? No idea why but it worked for him.

Have you considered which way the wind is blowing? Smells are difficult to sense if they are down wind of you. With the wind blowing into your face any scent will be directed towards you making it easier to detect. Wind is also responsible for making objects move or lights to shimmer.

A new investigator may find the sight of leaves

moving enough to make them jump but
seasoned hunters will allow for it. Sounds daft
but you will be surprised what can spook you
when you are in that state of mind. The whole
mentality changes and you focus on things that
you would not normally pay attention to so
when something does go bump, even of an
innocent nature, your mind can jump!

Chapter 13

Crossing over

Why does a spirit choose to not cross over to the next level? Why hang round? Opinions on this matter vary. For some it is the way in which they died, if it was sudden and completely unexpected like a car crash or murder, then there is an element of disorientation. This in itself would lead to a confusion of what is supposed to happen next. If they had unfinished business or weren't ready to let go you may find that is why they hover or linger around. In the event of suicide there may be regret or fear of judgement on their actions. If they have been responsible for dreadful deeds against fellow mankind the fear of judgement could also be the cause.

If it has been the result of an untimely death then the chances are there is business to finish, perhaps a last message to someone living. It is best to let them have their say and then they can move on. With suicide there can be overwhelming remorse and a spirit could be desperate for forgiveness from those they left behind. Once they know that they are forgiven then they can continue their way to the next stage of their journey. When dealing with the spirit of a murderer then you may find they are the nasty type of spirit. Their fear of being judge or going to hell may be the very thing stopping them from crossing.

 With the others it is safe to communicate yourself or be in the presence of a medium who can help you by acting as a go between, after all, that is what they do. When it comes to the later, call in a medium or investigation team who trained to deal with these things. It is best not to try yourself, things could go very pear shaped indeed. It is possible that a member of the clergy is best suited for the task in hand. Never take chances! I will say this again, if you feel or think there may be the involvement of a demon, call a priest. DO NOT TACKLE THIS! It requires years of specialist training that clergymen undertake. Mediums,psychics and investigators do not tend to have this sort of training. Leave it to the big guns!

Chapter 14

Final thoughts

The first thing we want to do when out ghost hunting is have fun. The passion for it will soon fade if we don't. The second reason is to find evidence that ghosts and the paranormal are real or not. It is an adventure of discovery. We all like a good scare and what better way to go about it.

 Research and investigations with like minded people or friends, the social side of events it is all part of being a team. To get together at a meeting or share a drink in the pub after events is an aspect of being in a society were you can relax and be happy. Sharing stories and happenings and recounting tales is all part of the fun, it creates a sense of belonging that we all need from time to time.

The other side of the coin is the research and information gathered during a site visit. It all comes together to help people understand the world we live in and its mysteries. We don't need to be afraid of ghosts just understand them and what it is all about. It has been the lack of understanding that has caused much confusion in mankind's existence. From the witch hunts of old to the treatment of disease, lack of knowledge can be the route of all evil.

It is only through education and knowledge that we progress. To investigate is knowledge even if it results in us following a different set of beliefs. Without People taking chances and acquiring information the human race will never develop. We would end up n a place were we believe what we are told and nothing different. That would lead to a failure on the part of man and nothing ever being developed.

So you may be just out looking for a ghost or quick scare but what you are really doing is developing the mind into asking questions, looking for answers and above all not taking anything for granted. When we blindly do as we are told without question then we are no more than sheep in a flock, this is not us. If people ask enough questions then science has to sit up and take notice. It can no longer ignore a situation or pass off an under researched answer.

There is something in the subject we just don't know for sure. In the world we live in, we require proof of a subject, not just believe without tangible evidence.

For centuries there have been accounts of the unnatural, ghosts and paranormal events and yet no evidence in the eyes of science. Not yet anyway. I do believe that evidence will surface and true explanations will be discovered, until then I will keep searching and hunting for evidence.

Some of the best stories and hauntings have no solid evidence yet they have been experienced by many, take the story of Winchester house? Many say that there are ghosts but it has never been proved, or disproved.

San Jose Winchester mystery house.

Lady Winchester was convinced she was haunted
by the victims killed by the firearms her family
company made. That is probably why she built the
house in a very ecaptic way. So she could avoid
them!

Check list
Items we need to investigate

1. Notebook and pen
2. Camera
3. Sound recorder
4. Back pack
5. First aid kit
6. Compass
7. Spare batteries
8. Water to drink
9. Flashlights

Optional

EMF meter
EVP meter
Thermometer

Useful to have

Map of site
Spirit board
Divining rods
Chalk
Walkie talkies
Spare clothes
Cell phone
USb charger for the car

Team members

1

2

3

4

5

Date

Location

Notes.

Time

Weather

Outside temp

Indoor temp

Record any events, sightings or feelings even if
they seem unimportant. They may be useful
when cross checking or back research.

Record your notes on the
following pages. It helps to
keep records together.

Notes.

Notes.

Notes.

Notes.

Remember have fun!

Happy hunting

Drew Martin

freefromdistraction.com
life journey61@gmail.com
fbme@spooky61
Vancouver Island Paranormal Investigation and
Research Society.

9 781723 875557